The
Helen Forrester
Walk

K.E. Rickard

First published 1987 by Countyvise Limited, 1 & 3 Grove Road, Rock Ferry, Birkenhead, Wirral, Merseyside L42 3XS.

Copyright © K.E. Rickard, 1987.

Photoset and printed by Birkenhead Press Limited, 1 & 3 Grove Road, Rock Ferry, Birkenhead, Merseyside L42 3XS.

ISBN 0 907768 13 X

Foreword

I hope that Mr. Rickard's book will encourage both visitors and residents to walk in Liverpool and appreciate the many fine Victorian buildings still to be seen in it. The handsome residences of the south end are falling into decay, but still give indication of their original charm in a sweep of steps, a pillared portico or a pair of brass doorknobs; young people should see them before the whole district is overtaken by creeping red brick. Princes Park and Sefton Park are two, great healthy lungs full of fresh air for children to enjoy. The City cannot always afford to take care of them as well as it might wish, but they are full of wildlife and a birdwatcher's paradise. Many people bewail our empty River Mersey; they remember it when it was full of shipping. But it is an ill wind that blows nobody any good and we can now walk by our river in a number of places; and it is clean enough for fish to be returning to it, a lovely place to sail a little boat.

When I was a child, pushing a yet smaller child along in a battered pram, I explored my city. It was interesting, there was always something new to discover, and it kept me sane.

Helen Forrester

Helen Forrester Walk

Helen Forrester spent her childhood with her middle-class parents and a steadily-increasing number of brothers and sisters in their comfortable country-town home in south-west England.

In the early 1930's, shortly after the birth of a seventh child, disaster struck.

For Helen and the other children there was no warning. They were simply informed that a thing called "bankruptcy" had happened to their father, making it necessary for the family to leave their home and move to Liverpool; immediately, and without luggage or other possessions.

The family were to live in the Liverpool slums throughout the 30's and Helen later vividly recorded her teenage life there in the best-selling books *Twopence to Cross the Mersey* and *Minerva's Stepchild (Liverpool Miss* in paperback).

Part 1 of this guide briefly re-tells her story, while Part 2 invites the reader to step into Helen's shoes and to visit the streets, buildings and sights she knew. Corresponding numbers are shown against places of interest in both parts and on the accompanying map. The distance covered by the walk is six miles.

Reference numbers 1-10 **in Part 2** correspond with those in Part 1 and the map. Numbers 11-22 **in Part 2** refer to the map only.

1. Helen's Story

The arrival of the family at Lime Street Station (1) was a nightmare Helen was never to forget. Not only was the family homeless and destitute — her mother was still weak from recent major surgery and had to be carried on a stretcher from train to waiting-room, where she lay on a bench, helpless and hardly conscious of what was happening.

Helen was later to learn that the family's financial misfortune, although partly due to the Great Depression, was largely a result of her parents' reckless extravagance and the foolhardy borrowing with which they had attempted to feed it. Her father had brought his family to Liverpool in the hope that they would be able to make a new life in the great city; in reality they were soon to realise that they had been caught in a trap of seemingly endless poverty with its resultant cold, hunger, dirt, humiliation and despair.

Their situation was pitiable. A few years later, even victims of savage Nazi evictions were allowed one well-packed suitcase per adult; the Forrester family had as their sole luggage one blanket, three baby nappies and a feeding-bottle, with just enough money left to pay for one week's lodgings and the taxi — necessitated by Mrs. Forrester's condition — to go to them.

When Mr. Forrester hurried out of the station to search for somewhere for the family to stay, it was Helen, as the eldest child, who was left to look after her mother and the baby, and to give what comfort and encouragement she could to the fretting, crying children.

For four agonizing hours they awaited his return. Dusk was already falling as he entered the waiting-room, exhausted from rushing from one seedy lodging-house to another, only to be refused as soon as he had mentioned his family of seven children. Eventually he had been offered, for seven days only, two of the shabbiest, filthiest rooms he had ever seen; worn down with fatigue and worry, he had gladly accepted.

The next morning Mr. Forrester sought out the appropriate office to apply for Parish relief. At the end of a humiliating interview he was granted the amount officially considered enough to keep two adults and seven children alive — £2.3/- per week (equal to £34.40 in today's money). For the foreseeable future, the family were not going to have enough to eat, and in winter were going to suffer terribly, with little money left for coal and none at all for clothing. When he broke the news to Helen and her mother, they were dismayed to the point of tears. The other children were told nothing.

Lime Street Station (1).

St. Margaret's Church. The school can be seen behind (3).

The corner of Upper Canning Street (2).

After a few day's rest, Mrs. Forrester felt a little stronger and undertook to go out to seek more permanent accommodation about one mile south of the city centre. Everywhere, she found the same attitude against large families, and had almost given up hope when she found a landlady willing to take them in at an exorbitant rent of 27/- (£21.60) per week. Although she did ask to be shown the rooms, this was a mere formality; they were so dreadful, she could hardly bring herself to look at them.

On the day the Forrester family climbed the 64 stairs of the house, in Upper Canning Street (2), to take possession of the top two bedrooms and one attic room, they found themselves in the midst of almost unbelievable squalor. The floors were only partly covered by remnants of linoleum over the filthy boards; the walls and ceilings were black with age, smoke and neglect; the iron beds were rusty and broken, the mattresses filthy and stinking. The "living-room/kitchen" had only one amenity — the usual open-fire bedroom grate. The lavatory was on the first floor, three floors below, as was the bathroom, the sole usefulness of which was its water tap. Later, the family was to discover with horror that the house was infested with bugs.

In the days, weeks and months that followed, the family adopted routines that helped them to come to terms with their sudden fall from middle-class comfort to pauper-class destitution. Four of the children who were of school age were enrolled at a local Church school (3). Mr. Forrester spent his time between the labour exchange — hoping to be offered employment as a clerk although over-age for this to be a real possibility — and the public library in Windsor Street (4). Mrs. Forrester soon began to work as a freelance saleswoman — for wages that were largely swallowed up by the necessity to maintain a presentable appearance, as the rest of the family's clothes became increasingly begrimed and tattered.

Only Helen — to whom school had always been the greatest joy — was tied down to the comfortless rooms: she was ordered to keep house and to look after the youngest child and the baby. Her vigorous protests that this was illegal as she was still of school age, were peremptorily brushed aside.

In the event there was very little housework to be done. Without bedding there were no beds to be made; there was no cooking as there was only one old saucepan — for heating water on the open fire; house-cleaning was impossible without brushes, brooms, dusters, soap; there were no changes of clothes, so little washing could be done — with cold water only; for shopping, Helen would be handed a shilling or so to buy bread, margarine, potatoes, and — all too frequently — cigarettes for her addicted parents.

Disgusted by the dirty, smelly house, Helen took her grubby charges on protracted walks in the fresh — and only slightly colder — air of the city streets. When a friendly neighbour presented her with an ancient wreck of a pram for the baby, her mother was predictably shocked, but she had begun to accept her loss of status and grudgingly allowed Helen to keep it. In any case, Helen was by then as ragged as her "chariot", as Mrs. Forrester called the pram. She was still dressed in the school-uniform gymslip, now shiny with dirt, that she had worn on the family's arrival in Liverpool, but she had had to give the blouse to a school-going sister and replace it with an old, ragged cardigan of her mother's. Her shoes had been exchanged for a pair of hopelessly worn plimsolls bought for a couple of pence from the local pawnbroker. Her legs were permanently bare and in summer she was often to go barefoot.

The Rose Garden, Princes Park (5).

Princes Park (5).

The chariot proved to be a great boon. It allowed Helen to push baby and child as far as Princes Park (5) and, at times, on even longer walks to the Palm House in Sefton Park (6), just to be warm for a little while — hidden under the palms. She found that while pushing she could read a book — borrowed from the public library — placed on the pram cover. In Princes Park she was befriended by an elderly Lebanese gentleman with whom she would sit on a bench in the rose garden near the lake. His philosophical attitude to misfortune, and his assurance to Helen that her reading was in itself an excellent form of self-education, made it possible for her to overcome the despair that constantly threatened her.

The chariot was also useful for taking back to the house all kinds of objects that Helen found in the streets — newspaper, twigs, string, old boots. Anything that could be burned would bring a little extra warmth into the life of the family. The old pram did, however, prevent her from entering the museum in William Brown Street one day (7); it was far too shabby to be allowed through the sacred portals.

Eventually, school inspectors called at the house, and as a result, to Helen's delight and her mother's annoyance, she had to join her brothers and sisters in school, while her mother stayed at home. Unfortunately, Helen's rescue by the Education Act had come too late; within six weeks she reached the age of fourteen and her schooldays were over.

The Palm House,
Sefton Park (6)

11

William Brown Street Museum (7).

The family's fortunes took a turn for the better when, in the city centre one day, an observant police inspector noticed the old public school tie Mr. Forrester was still wearing although he was otherwise in rags. By chance, the inspector had attended the same school. He soon learned the story behind the rags, and was subsequently able to persuade the City Council to offer Mr. Forrester a clerical job.

On the strength of his being once again in employment, Mr. Forrester was able to rent a house (8), which was an improvement as there were no stairs to climb, no other tenants to share the toilet (although this was outside), and there was a proper kitchen range and a gas cooker. On the debit side, there was very little furniture; Helen's bed had to be an old door supported by bricks at each corner, while old paint cans had to be us d as chairs. Bugs still added to the miseries of life.

In spite of the catastrophe — largely caused by their lack of sense of responsibility — that had blighted their lives and those of their children, Helen's parents did not change their ways. From the start, they had habitually put themselves in debt to local shopkeepers, and had continually looked on pawning anything, even essentials such as overcoats, as a solution to financial difficulties. Now, with money once again jingling in his pocket, Mr. Forrester started to frequent the local pubs; this in turn made Mrs. Forrester feel justified in

12

paying weekly visits to the cinema, while the house reeked from their now unrestrained cigarette smoking. They bought, on the "never-never", a suite of expensive lounge furniture and curtains for all the windows. Predictably, they failed to keep up the weekly repayments and the goods were re-possessed.

Helen had believed that the troubles of all the members of the family would fade away once her father left the ranks of the unemployed. Now he had a good job but there were still no blankets, no extra coal or food, no clothes for her. The realisation that there was no longer anything to look forward to, shocked her into a sense of such hopelessness, life seemed no longer worth living.

The Pier Head (9).

One evening she took the baby in the chariot to the Pier Head (9). She stepped over the chain fence and looked down at the still, dark water below; it offered peace, an end to privation, cold, hunger, fear and humiliation. For a while she gazed into the depths, her mind in turmoil, and it was this hesitation that saved her life. A seaman who had been watching her had realised her intention and had crept up behind her. As she jumped, he caught her shoulders and dress, and pulled her to safety.

She did not tell her parents about the incident. That another human being had cared enought to save her had a sobering effect; she was not going to make another attempt.

From the beginning, Helen had dreamed of resuming her interrupted education by attending night-school. Her parents had always refused point-blank to allow this on the grounds that they had

13

no money for fees, and even their newly-improved circumstances did nothing to change their attitude. So Helen plucked up her courage and presented them with a fait-accompli by enrolling at a night-school. When she dared to tell them, they were furious but, probably prompted by conscience, finally relented and gave her, if not their blessing, at least the necessary half-crown.

Helen was behind in her studies; but her enthusiasm for learning and the kindness of her teachers resulted in rapid progress. One subject she studied — shorthand — was to prove invaluable to her later.

At about this time, a deaconess connected with the Church school attended by Helen's brothers and sisters, heard about the plight of the family and, in particular, all about Helen. She was most concerned that a girl "of good family" should be living without proper food, clothing, bedding or other necessities. When she learned that a charity with offices (10) in the city centre had a vacancy for an office girl of Helen's age, she arranged an interview for her. She had assumed, cannily, that Helen's parents would be opposed to her going out to work — she was too useful as unpaid housemaid and nanny — and only told them afterwards. In the course

The "Charity" (10).

of the ensuing angry scene with Helen, they craftily pointed out that, in any case, she could hardly attend an interview in the only clothes she had — the out-grown gymslip, mere remnants of the cardigan, and tennis shoes with no toes — let alone go to work in them. Helen's mother was, however, finally persuaded to write to an old school-friend with wealthy parents, who immediately sent her a complete set of used, but serviceable clothes.

Working for the Charity was no bed of roses for Helen. She worked long, stressful hours for a tiny wage, almost all of which was taken by her mother, leaving little for lunches or clothes. She had to walk to and from work as she didn't have the twopenny tram fare unable to pay for shoe repairs, she would often arrive with rain-sodden feet. Her living conditions improved very little over the years but she maintained her loyalty to the Charity in the hope of being trained as a qualified social worker.

It was not until well after the outbreak of war in 1939 that, after much soul-searching, Helen left the Charity and went to work, at a living wage, as a secretary in a nationalised industry outside the city. Passing through the door of her new office on that first morning, she was — at last — leaving behind the world of nightmare and entering into a new, normal life.

The war, with its full employment and increased wages, had hastened the happy ending to this part of Helen's story; but it did not spare her a full share of the world-wide heartbreak it brought in its wake. Helen's wartime experiences are dramatically related in her final autobiographical books *By the Waters of Liverpool* and *Lime Street at Two*.

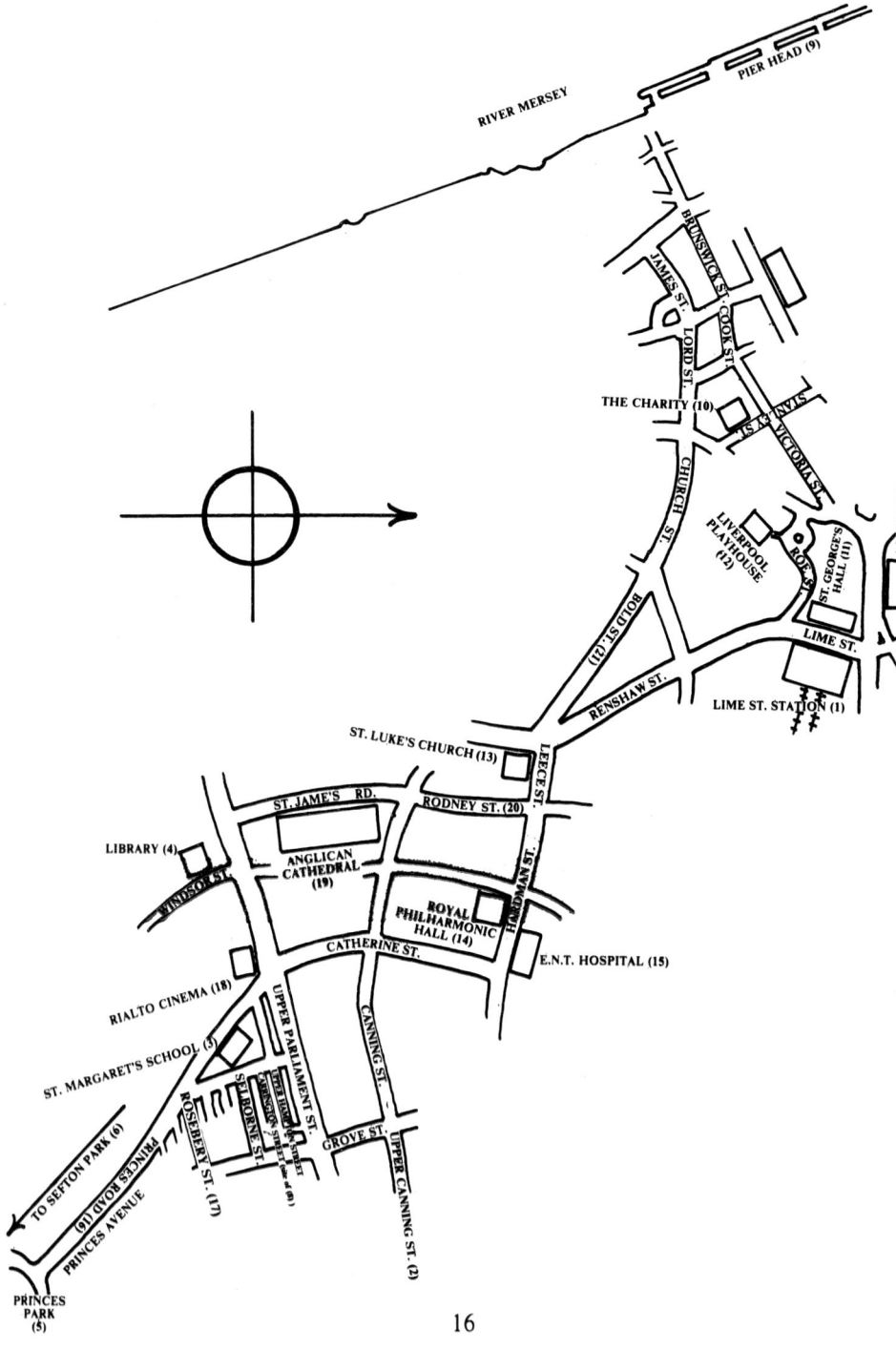

RIVER MERSEY

PIER HEAD (9)

WILLIAM BROWN ST. MUSEUM (7)

BRUNSWICK ST.

COOK ST.

JAMES ST.

LORD ST.

CHURCH ST.

THE CHARITY (10)

S. JOHN'S

VICTORIA ST.

BOLD ST. (21)

LIVERPOOL PLAYHOUSE (12)

ROE ST.

ST. GEORGE'S HALL (11)

LIME ST.

RENSHAW ST.

LIME ST. STATION (1)

ST. LUKE'S CHURCH (13)

LEECE ST.

ST. JAME'S RD.

RODNEY ST. (20)

HARDMAN ST.

LIBRARY (4)

WINDSOR ST.

ANGLICAN CATHEDRAL (19)

ROYAL PHILHARMONIC HALL (14)

E.N.T. HOSPITAL (15)

CATHERINE ST.

RIALTO CINEMA (18)

UPPER PARLIAMENT ST.

CANNING ST.

ST. MARGARET'S SCHOOL (3)

ROSEBERY ST. (17)

ST. BRIDE'S STREET (Site of 8)

GROVE ST.

UPPER CANNING ST. (2)

TO SEFTON PARK (6)

PRINCES ROAD (16)

PRINCES AVENUE

PRINCES PARK (5)

16

2. The Walk

Reference numbers 1-10 correspond with those in Part 1 and the map. Numbers 11-22 refer to the map only.

Lime Street Station (1), the scene of Helen's and her family's unhappy arrival in Liverpool, is a logical starting point for a walk from the city centre to the sites of Helen's former slum homes. The out and return routes take us past vistas and along streets largely unchanged since she and her family walked them daily, in all weathers, ragged and ill-shod.

The view from the entrance to Lime Street Station is the same today as it was when Helen, awaiting the return of her father, slipped out of the waiting-room to look out for him. In spite of her anxiety she noted the colonnaded St. George's Hall (11) opposite, and, away to the right, the sweep of steps in front of the William Brown Street Museum (7).

Cross straight over Lime Street into St. George's Place, and turn left into Roe Street. Ahead, in Williamson Square, stands the famous Liverpool Playhouse (12) where Helen spent many happy evenings, her ticket paid for by one of the Charity's wealthier benefactors. Return to Lime Street, continuing south into Renshaw Street.

At the top of Renshaw Street stands St. Luke's Church (13), now a shell through wartime bombing. Its flight of stone steps offered a haven of rest to Helen on two occasions when she sank down onto them suffering from semi-starvation and exhaustion. The second occurrence was while she was working for the Charity, and heralded a complete nervous breakdown.

Bear left into Leece Street, then Hardman Street. On the right, on the corner of Hope Street, the Royal Philharmonic Hall (14) was rebuilt in 1939 after having been burned down in 1933. The fire was "enjoyed" by two little witnesses — Helen's young brothers.

A little further along Hardman Street is the Ear, Nose and Throat Hospital (15), where Helen was examined by a specialist and found to be suffering from advanced malnutrition. His subsequent fury with Helen's mother could be clearly heard through the closed door of his office. She emerged white-faced and obviously shaken; it had never occurred to her that she had been depriving her children of vital food by her compulsive spending on unnecessary luxuries.

Turn right into Catherine Street, then left into Canning Street whose 3-storey terraces are similar to the house in Upper Canning Street (2), an extension to Canning Street, in which the Forrester family first lived in Liverpool. All the Upper Canning Street houses have since been demolished.

St. George's Hall (11)

Liverpool Playhouse (12).

18

Ear, Nose and Throat Hospital (15).

St. Luke's Church (13).

Turn right into Grove Street, then right again into the wide boulevard Upper Parliament Street. The Forresters' rented house was in Carrington Street (8) which ran parallel to "Upper Parly" Street on the south side between Upper Hampton and Selborne Streets, but has now completely disappeared.

At the crossroads turn left into Princes Road (16). The school on this corner, St. Margaret's, is the Church school (3) attended by the Forrester children. Rosebery Street (17), where the Forresters lived in their later years in Liverpool, is a turning on the left.

The dual-carriageway Princes Road — beyond this point known as Princes Road on the south side and Princes Avenue on the north — leads straight to Princes Park (5), the footpaths of which were so often scuffed by the tyre-less wheels of the chariot.

Those who have the time can pass through the whole length of Princes Park into adjoining Sefton Park and its Palm House (6). This detour adds an extra $1\frac{1}{2}$ miles to the walk.

Commence the return walk via Princes Road/Avenue, and on reaching the Upper Parliament Street intersection, turn left. The Rialto Cinema and Dance Hall (18), frequently mentioned in the Helen Forrester books, stood on this corner. They were destroyed by fire during rioting a few years ago.

A short distance along Upper Parliament Street, on Windsor Street, is the public library (4) which brought so much comfort to Helen and her family.

Cross Upper Parliament Street into St. James Road and pass the Anglican Cathedral (19) in which Helen was confirmed, wearing a borrowed dress and hiding her gloveless hands in the sleeves.

Carry on into Rodney Street (20), Liverpool's "Harley Street". Helen loved its solid architecture and passed through slowly, taking in its peace and orderliness in such contrast to the teeming slum in which she was forced to live.

Turn left into Hardman Street/Leece Street, pass St. Luke's Church — on the left-hand side this time — and bear right into Bold Street (21). In this fashionable street the urchin Helen and her chariot. passed an old schoolfriend on a visit to Liverpool out shopping with her mother. They gave one glance, and turned away in disgust. Humiliated beyond words, Helen watched them go, her eyes filled with tears.

Continue into Church Street, then Lord Street and James Street, turn right into Goree, left at Brunswick Street to the Pier Head (9), the site of Helen's suicide attempt.

Return by Brunswick Street past Liverpool's well-known Town Hall (22) at the end of Castle Street on the left, noting Minerva

Princes Road (16).

Roseberry Street (17).

21

Canning Street.

Anglican Cathedral (19).

Rodney Street (20).

Bold Street (21).

perched on the dome. Continue on Cook Street, then Victoria Street. The offices of the Charity (10) — the Liverpool Personal Service Society — occupy no. 34 Stanley Street which crosses Victoria Street about half-way along. From the end of Victoria Street, Lime Street Station can be seen again, ahead and to the right of St. John's Garden.

Liverpool Town Hall (22).